Open Hearts - Open Minds

Working Therapeutically with displaced, separated,

unaccompanied persons including children …

By Cesca Pellegrini (Pen Name) 2011, 2023 ©

Research Project from 2011 - Updates included

Introduction & Abstract

Methodology

Research Findings – Safeguarding and Promoting the Welfare of Separated Children

Research Findings – Training for foster Carers

Conclusion

Bibliography

Introduction

Separated persons including children arriving in the United Kingdom (UK) from their respective countries of origin are in need of support and protection by the host nation. Depending on their age and level of support needs, it is the responsibility of Adults and Children's Services to make provision for their needs to be met.

Social workers have statutory and ethical responsibilities in safeguarding and promoting the welfare of displaced, separated, unaccompanied, persons and refugees - where certain legal criteria are met.

The original research project I undertook over a decade ago - has been updated post the Covid-19 era, as my reflections on being raised in the western world, with a multicultural immigrant perspective has coloured my reflections, in ways I could not have imagined a decade ago.

When I first undertook my research project over a decade ago, I never imagined that the world scene would have altered so

drastically. Multiple military and political coups, a man of East
African, Punjabi speaking son of immigrants as the British Prime
Minister, several assassinations of world leaders, earthquakes in
Turkey, Syria, Morocco, tsunamis and floods in Pakistan and
Lebanon, 'terrorist attacks', labelled such by different countries,
national wars such as the wars fought byUkraine and Russia, civil
war based on different ideological faiths, persecution of faith groups
such as the Rohingyas, the Uyghurs and the Buddhists monks, as
well as indiscriminate killings of Christians - has resulted in
displacement of thousands, refugees fleeing for reasons of
personal, political and spiritual warfare - are dispersed worldwide
wherever and whichever country opens their hearts and minds to
them.

Since undertaking my research project over a decade ago - I
suffered from burnout, hospitalisation and the stigma, isolation,
targeted harassment and ridicule faced from ignorant ex family and
former friends and former colleagues, brought home to me that by

and large - Closed Hearts & Closed Minds - is simply a way of life among the indifferent.

My purpose in updating my research paper to ensure that it remains relevant - is simply to add a note at the beginning and end, offering a social commentary on how things may or may not have ameliorated for the better.

Having separated from my forever love and stepson - both of whom I never got to meet in person due to the war in the Middle East, gave me a greater sense of empathy for those in similar positions - a perspective that I had not known prior to undertaking my research project.

I dedicate the findings of this research to those with Open Hearts & Open Minds....

As an advocate of alternative medicine and therapies - I simply offer a simple remedy which is organic and can be used as a tool for all manner of physical and emotional healing of trauma.... The recipe below can be adapted, and used if there are no contraindications to natural medicine.

Organic Pink Solitaire Rose Petal Tea

A handful of freshly picked organic rose petals, washed in water.

Placed in a pot of water, simmer in the oven for an hour or on the hob with honey.

Other spices such as fresh mint, vanilla, apple, lemon, and fresh coffee can be added if you prefer to flavour the tea with such organic ingredients.

The Organic Rose Petal Tea can be had with or without milk.

Intuition guided me to make the tea, without any idea of its health benefits - I researched the health benefits after a few hours of sipping the tea, as the floodgates opened up and years of post traumatic stress, bereavement grief and sadness began to pour out of me from the depths of the iceberg.

On completing my research I found that rose petals are often used in tea and tinctures as a remedy for grief and menopausal symptoms, the bereavement of child birthing opportunities.

A daily cup of Rose Petal Tea from the garden proved to be gentler and more soothing and deeper than any homoeopathy, herbal or Big Pharma recipe.

Grief is often deep, hidden and locked within the hearts, minds and physical anatomy of displaced, separated, and refugee persons. I offer this recipe simply as a gift…which one is free to try or not, once undertaking your own research first.

The sad reality is that monitoring the standard of care that refugees, displaced and separated persons including children receive when placed in care.

This paper explores my personal research findings, undertaken as a Postgraduate in Law, whilst undertaking a Masters Degree, as to whether the training available to carers is effective in terms of improving their practice and improving outcomes for displaced, unaccompanied, traumatised asylum and refugees persons including children.

The original research I undertook was in relation to children, however, the principles and much of the finding of the research apply equally to adults, immigrants, and colleagues and neighbours from countries worldwide.

Overall, the research findings strongly suggest that despite positive training course evaluations by foster carers in preparation for them to care for other people's children, their training does not produce better outcomes for foster children. In light of these findings, this paper makes suggestions of ways research may strategically influence those responsible for commissioning future training and concludes with suggestions of subject areas for future research.

Key words: 'unaccompanied asylum seeking minors', 'refugees', 'forced migration', 'separated children', 'foster care', 'foster carers', 'foster carer training'.

INTRODUCTION

As a disillusioned ex-therapeutic worker, in the community, my initial interest in the area of social work was first ignited whilst on my first student social work placement in a team supporting refugees within the public sector.

In that role I worked on behalf of young people from the ages of 15-22, as well as foster carers, predominantly from the Middle East, and their supervising workers.

Reading articles by Ravi Kohli, (Kohli 2008, Kohli & Mather 2003), motivated an inner change and I began to appreciate that whilst separated children have needs and strengths similar to the general population of looked after children, they have additional needs borne out of their particular experiences relating to migration from their countries of origin and resettlement into a new country.

As a former trained therapeutic carer, my personal interest in therapeutic commissioned work led me to ponder whether foster carers and parents were being sufficiently grounded pre and post-approval to meet the challenges of caring for separated children. It also helped me to appreciate that the same questions could be asked of colleagues, neighbours and the community at large - with some much ignorance and prejudice it is a miracle that the broken world has not annihilated itself.

By declaring my personal and professional interests in my research project at the outset and in the spirit of openness and integrity, important aspects of therapeutic work research ethics, I seek to demonstrate and acknowledge an understanding of the dangers of 'researcher bias'.

Having made a conscious effort to remain open hearted and open minded and accept whatever the research findings may reveal - I had no idea, that over a decade on from this research that some of its findings would still resonate with me, as a third generation immigrant, which is ingrained in my ethnic, spiritual and social dna.

Prior to addressing the methodological process undertaken and presenting the findings of the literature review, I will present my research statement and define the various terms used therein.

Research Statement

In the process of formulating my research statement constituted a work in progress and throughout the research project I continually revised and re-worded the statement, having in mind the overall purpose of my literature review.

My research statement appears below in italics: -

Effective avenues of foster carers' training related to caring for separated children on their arrival to the UK: A review of research findings.

The terms 'foster carers' or 'foster parents' are used interchangeably throughout this research project. They refer to

hose individuals who have undertaken basic pre-approval training
ınd subsequently been approved as foster carers.

n England fostering services are governed by The Fostering
Services Regulations 2002 and foster carers are required to meet
:ertain minimum standards of care. It had been my original intention
ɔ use the term 'training' to encompass formal training courses run
ıy fostering agencies and other organisations, however, research
ndings led me to widen my perspective to include individual
raining within a foster carer's home, group work, joint training with
.ocial workers, training via supervision and informal training by
ɔster children.

n using the term 'effective' training, I am referring to training that
levelops the knowledge base and skills of foster carers in order to
mprove their practice and improve outcomes for separated children.

The United Nations Convention on the Rights of the Child 1989 defines a child as an individual under the age of eighteen, unless the host nation defines them otherwise (Martin & Curran 2007).

It is important to note that there exist different cultural and legal concepts of 'childhood' throughout the world, and that in the UK, the term 'child' refers to an individual under the age of eighteen and so this is the definition I will be sticking to for the purposes of this research paper.

The age of a child or young person is a significant factor because it determines the kind of social care provisions available, including foster care. For the purposes of this research project, I have limited my discussion to children and young people who have been 'accommodated' under S.20 Children Act 1989 (CA) and have the legal status of being 'looked after' by their respective local authorities and are in foster care. I recognise that this may exclude those young people between the ages of 16 and 18 who are deemed to be 'children in need' under S.17 CA 1989 but who are not placed in foster care.

The term 'separated children' encompasses children and young people who are "...outside of their country of origin and separated from both parents or their previous legal or customary primary caregiver...", (Ni Raghallaigh & Gilligan 2010, 226) a citation taken from the Separated Children in Europe Programme 2004. It had been my original intention to use the terms 'unaccompanied asylum seeking children' and 'refugees'. In opting to use the term 'separated children, ' I noted that the politically correct terminology equated with using the term 'separated children'.

Ethically and from an immigration perspective, the term 'unaccompanied' carries a very narrow interpretation. Iit places the focus on minors who on their arrival to the UK are alone without their parents or caregivers. Although 'unaccompanied' also encompasses those children and young people who may have been separated from their parents or caregivers on route it does not encompasses those children and young people who arrive in the UK 'accompanied', but with adults who may have exploited or intend to exploit them for the purposes of human trafficking (Bhabha & Finch 2006).

Whilst it is outside the scope of my dissertation to include an in-depth discussion of child trafficking, for reasons of domestic servitude, temporary marriages, sham marriages, sexual exploitation and related issues, I have chosen to use the term 'separated children' in-order to be all encompassing.

From a child centred perspective, the term 'separated children' is preferable because it emphasises the "...crucial fact of children's separation from their parents and the powerful effect that this has on their welfare..." (Martin & Curran, 2007:444).

In acknowledging that the term 'separated children' gives no indication as to legal status in terms of whether an individual is seeking asylum, has been granted leave to remain or has been accorded full refugee status.

The term 'separated children', (which denotes a 'group'), I am conscious that such children do not constitute a homogenous group, but that each child or young person is a unique individual in their own right.

At the time of undertaking my initial research, the political and social climate in relation to immigration was contentious, over a decade on the situation remains the same.

In everyday vocabulary speech terms such as 'asylum seeker' and 'refugee', are often used interchangeably (albeit incorrectly), as if they mean the same thing (Okitkpi & Aymer 2006). In a recent research project led by Chase (2009) exploring the emotional well-being of young people seeking asylum in England it states that "...being defined as an 'asylum-seeker' and the consequent stigma this invoked was ubiquitous in many young people's accounts of their lives in the UK..." (Chase 2009, 7).

In using the term 'separated children' throughout my research paper, when citing other researchers and authors, I will include the terms that they use, such as 'unaccompanied asylum seeking children', 'asylum seekers' and 'refugees'.

As with the use of most terms, I accept that one's legal, political, sociological or other perspective may have a bearing on the choice of terms used, however, in this respect, I make no judgments of others.

The methodological process of my research project and the unexpected challenges I faced along the way, are documented below.

METHODOLOGY

Good research practice and research ethics adhere to the following fundamental principles: that research should do no harm, that consent of its participants should be voluntary, that confidentiality should be respected throughout the process, and that the process should be conducted with integrity, which includes the manner in which the findings are analysed and presented (Denscombe 2007). In relation to social work research,

The Code of Ethics for Social Work states that "...social work researchers have a duty to maintain an active, personal and disciplined ethical awareness..." (The British Association of Social Workers, (BASW) 2002, 14). In undertaking this research project I was also bound by the policies of the Higher Education establishment, and as a result I was not permitted to undertake any direct fieldwork research of my own.

The epistemological and ontological approach, used by me, includes a review of research that reflects both interpretive constructivist and positivist research methods (Bryman 2008).

Although some of the studies that I reference utilise both qualitative

and quantitative research methods, overall, my preference for using

studies based on qualitative methods was linked to its

appropriateness of exploring the personal experiences of separated

children and foster carers.

Difficulties in drawing conclusions and making generalisations from

research, from the personal experiences of individuals, and the

limitation of qualitative research, meant that I grappled with how to

present the findings of my research initially. Overall, the overarching

theme of therapeutic work

is about understanding and relating to people as individuals on a

human to human level and seeking to offer therapeutic support.

Throughout the research project I located an abundance of peer

reviewed articles through various on-line database searches

conducted. The searches also uncovered other literature including books and internet reports which served as background information to my subject area.

Despite the wealth of information available on the subject of training foster carers, the lack of research linking this training to separated and displaced persons, including children, was a gap that needed to be addressed.

This was also noted in the research by Hek, who states that "relatively little research exists that explores the fostering of unaccompanied children either from their own perspective or from that of the foster carers supporting them" (Hek 2007, 109).

In an effort to build a bridge between the two, I made a decision to consider research studies which explored various avenues of foster carers' training and possible contributory factors which may have impacted positively or negatively on the effectiveness of training. From those studies I then looked at common themes which I felt could be transferred from those specific studies to foster carers' training in general (an exercise which I recognise involves a level of personal subjectivity). The discussion and research papers originate from various countries namely the UK, Ireland, Europe, Australia, Canada and the US dating from the 1980's up until 2010.

The majority of the research studies I examined contained detailed accounts of their methodological process – in selecting participants, the demographics of participants, data collection methods – such as interviews, questionnaires, observation methods, the process of obtaining voluntary and informed consent, and ethical issues. Other studies contained very little information about their methodological processes. Some of the research included was undertaken by those who were either employed by or had other interests in the organisation that funded the research. Although this did not lead me to question their findings, the apparent lack of independence may have impacted on the weight that I accorded them, when comparing their findings against evidence from other research findings.

Some studies included participants who were 'self selected', some included positivist research methods such as randomised control trials with a sample and a control group. There was one study which openly acknowledged that the foster children had been paid a small financial sum to participate in the study (Jackson 2009). While some may consider paid participation in research studies to be unethical and thus choose to exclude them, I decided otherwise. My reason for including this study was that it highlighted similar themes that separated children identified as being important to them, also highlighted as important by the studies with unpaid participants.

Starting Point

As a basis for starting my research project, I approached the British Adoption and Fostering Agency (BAAF) and Fostering Network to request permission to informally 'evaluate' the content of their respective training manuals – 'Fostering Unaccompanied Asylum Seeking and Refugee Children – A Training Course for Foster Carers' (Kidane & Amerena 2004) and 'The Skills to Foster' (Fostering Network). This preparatory work was useful in enabling me to identify themes related to foster carers' training and caring for separated children.

My reasons for selecting these publications were firstly that both BAAF and Fostering Network are widely known and respected within the field of fostering, the themes explored therein have been extensively researched and lastly, their training manuals are readily accessible to therapeutic and social workers.

Database Searches

The first step in locating relevant research resources involved conducting on-line database searches using various keywords. Using the ASIA database, I searched under keywords such as 'foster care' or 'foster carer'. This search brought up over 1,656 articles, 1,119 of which had been peer reviewed, from which I printed around 25 articles in full. A more advanced search using the terms 'foster care' and 'training' brought up around 148 items, 103 of which had been peer reviewed from which I printed out abstracts for 73 articles. From these abstracts I then printed out 7 articles in ull. The criteria I used in deciding whether or not to print out an entire article was based largely on whether my interest was sufficiently aroused to read on, having in mind how closely the article related to my research project. In looking at the abstracts and articles, I endeavoured to locate research whose findings indicated different perspectives on foster carer training.

The second step of on-line database searches using ASIA and SCOPUS related to searching for articles relating to separated children. One of my first searches using 'unaccompanied' as a key word brought up over 1,600 articles. I narrowed the search by using the term 'unaccompanied asylum seeking children' this search brought up around 27 articles. The term 'asylum seeking children' brought up around 114 articles. The term 'refugee' brought up over 1070 articles and 'separated children' brought up over 5,900 articles. In an effort to narrow the search yet further, I limited the search to social science publications and the English language, this then brought up 473 articles and it was from these searches combined that I printed out a further 32 articles in full. Whilst scanning the abstracts for each article I noticed some of the articles

had already come up in previous searches so I was able to quickly

discount any duplication. I recognise that I could have used other

on-line database search engines but as I had already gathered over

50 articles, I made the decision to examine what I had, before

considering whether or not it was necessary to use additional

database searches.

Towards the end of my research project I examined the research

resources and found that I had included findings drawn from over 48

research studies and other information from resources including

from 8 books, 2 training course publications, statutory guidance and

a Home Office Consultation Paper. I felt that the variety of resources

was a sufficient mix from different perspectives and thus did not

conduct further on-line database searches.

After assembling, yet prior to reading the articles I had selected, I

devised a 4 page questionnaire to use as a tool to systematically

record whether each research article related to direct fieldwork or consisted of a literature review, the methodological process, the main points of the article, its findings and how these related to other studies, my perspective of each article and any areas for future research. This task, laborious as it was subsequently proved to be extremely useful in identifying recurring themes, which formed the basic structure of my research. I organised folders with subject dividers – one relating to foster carers and training, one relating to separated children and another in respect of articles that I found interesting and wanted to explore further.

Originally, I compiled a folder ('miscellaneous') as I was not sure at first how to use the information found therein, however, these subsequently proved to be rich sources of information such as articles relating to cross cultural fostering (Brown et al 2009a, 2009b) and articles relating to spirituality and religion (Jackson et al 2009).

I located additional resources through on-line database searches using the Advanced Access sections of journals such as the British

Journal of Social Work, Child and Family and the Journal of International Migration. I also explored references to articles, books or websites that were cited by other researchers in their articles. Where certain articles were unavailable to the University I requested them through the inter-library loans request system. Having gathered my resources, I set about formulating a list of references. Although I did not appreciate it at the time, the list of references became a useful tool in its own right, by which means I was able to track the quantity and type of reading I had completed. Throughout the research project I made additions to and subtractions from the reference list of articles based on their relevance to my research theme and whether or not I had made use of the articles in my research project.

Facing Challenges

The first challenge, related to selecting and then defining my use of certain terminology in my research statement.

At the start of my dissertation project I thought foster carers' 'training' was composed of formal training courses offered by fostering agencies and organisations such as Fostering Network and BAAF. As the project progressed it soon became evident that I needed to widen my perspective. The research highlighted other additional avenues of training such as: one-to-one training through supervision sessions of foster carers and social workers; individual training offered within the foster carer's home, (Hampson et al 2003); training through shared experiences and co-learning, (Berridge 2005, Warman et al 2006) and informal training of foster carers by their foster children (Brown et al 2009a, 2009b).

The most difficult challenge I faced throughout the research project was choosing the most appropriate terms to use – 'unaccompanied asylum seeking children' and 'refugees' or 'separated children'. I oscillated between these terms for a considerable amount of time.

At the start of my research project it had been my intention to use the term 'unaccompanied asylum seeking children', however, I chose to use the term separated children after becoming aware of

its use in current research (Abunimah & Blower 2010, Fejen 2009,

Crawley 2009, Bokhari 2008, Martin & Curran 2007, Bhabha &

Finch 2006, Bhabha 2004).

Originally it had been my intention to discuss focus on foster carers

caring for the 'needs' of separated children. Shortly after the project

progressed, I realised that I had fallen into the trap of stereotyping

separated children as 'victims', focusing on deficits whilst

overlooking their strengths.

There were several studies that were instrumental in shifting my

focus from a needs perspective to a needs and resilience

perspective in relation to separated children (Fejen 2009, Ni

Raghallaigh & Gilligan 2009, Maegusuku-Hewitt et al 2009 and

Warwick et al 2006, Kohli 2008). Ni Raghallaigh & Gilligan consider

the portrayal of "...refugee children as either 'vulnerable' or 'resilient'

as over-simplistic.

nstead, for many, *both* vulnerability and resilience may be
*vident..." (2009, 227). Kohli aptly describes unaccompanied
asylum seeking children as "...survivors as well as victims of the
particular circumstances that have removed them from their roots..."
Kohli, 2008). The research I felt as if I had been gently steered
owards a more realistic perspective of separated children.

Research Ethics With Asylum Seekers – The Debate

Two thirds of the way through my research project, during one of the
many database searches, I came across an article relating to
research and ethics in relation to asylum seekers in Australia (Zion
et al 2010).

Zion et al argue against direct empirical research with asylum
seekers on the grounds of protecting the vulnerability of such
individuals, the challenges posed in obtaining informed consent and
the difficulties in establishing "...equitable research partnerships
between participants and researchers..." (2010, 51). Zion et al
suggest that evidence and testimonies could be gathered from other

agencies who work closely with asylum seekers such as health professionals and advocates.

In response, Bloom (2010) argues that denying asylum seekers the opportunities to participate in research would serve to 'silence' their voices despite evidence of other research which indicates a willingness on the part of some individuals to participate. Secondly, Bloom argues that a restriction against direct participation would be tantamount to treating asylum seekers as 'objects' rather than 'subjects' of research. Thirdly Bloom argues that the use of third party perspectives and testimonies instead of that of the asylum seekers themselves would be to deny such individuals "...a most basic human need to be recognised – that is to be heard and seen as a human..." (2010, 60).

Whilst recognising that the research undertaken by Zion et al (2010) related to asylum seeking adults in Australia (who were incarcerated), points raised by their research are pertinent to the general debate on research and ethics with asylum seeking children and young people.

Despite the various challenges posed in respect of research ethics and methodological processes, the potential power imbalance between participants and researchers and the vulnerabilities of such individuals, asylum seekers should be given the opportunity to give informed consent to participating in empirical research. It is my personal and professional opinion that to deny individuals the 'right' to participate in research that concerns them, no matter how well intentioned, is somewhat 'oppressive' and 'unethical' as it denies the voices of service users to be heard.

In relation to research and ethics with children and young people seeking asylum Thomas & Byford (2003) assert that any research undertaken should be "...sensitive and appropriate to avoid causing more harm to a vulnerable population..." (2003, 1400). In the interests of ethics and good practice, Thomas & Byford suggest obtaining informed consent from the children and young people and where appropriate those who have responsibilities for them, researchers informing participants of child protection responsibilities if they become concerned during the research for the safety or the participant or others, ensuring that robust data protection procedures are followed and the making of provisions of support and de-briefing for the participants and researchers (Thomas & Byford 2003).

After reading these articles, I reviewed some of the research studies to see how they 'measured' up against these good practice standards. I found that none of the studies explicitly made mention of child protection responsibilities of researchers towards the participants and very few studies mention the provision of debriefing as a means of supporting both the participants and researchers.

Thomas & Byford's suggestions brought home how important it is for researchers to adhere to good research practice and ethical guidelines, not only when carrying out research with separated children but generally, including research conducted with foster carers. The arguments in favour of and against direct empirical research with asylum seekers served to open my eyes and helped me appreciate the enormity of the task, in undertaking direct fieldwork with foster carers and separated children for the research project.

Undertaking the project helped me to become more aware of the diverse ethical and methodological challenges faced by researchers in undertaking research and in disseminating their findings.

Having concluded the methodological process of my research project, the research findings in respect of the effectiveness of foster carers' training in relation to caring for separated children is presented below.

RESEACH FINDINGS

Research indicates that separated children arrive in the UK with a host of complex needs. In order to safeguard and promote their welfare, foster carers need to be sufficiently grounded with a sound knowledge base of fostering, related theories such as child development, attachment, the impact of trauma and also parental skills in order to meet the challenges of caring for those separated from their families and who are outside of their respective countries of origin. Coming from a child centred perspective I have chosen to start with an exploration of the research findings in relation to separated children first before examining the research related to the effectiveness of foster carers' training.

Safeguarding and Promoting the Welfare of Separated Children

Universally, children and young people are in need of care and protection. Within the population of looked after children separated children have unique psychological and associated needs arising out of their experiences of flight and migration from their country of origin, separation from their caregivers and families and their legal immigration status in the UK (Abunimah & Blower 2010, Derluyn & Broekaert 2008, Maegusuku-Hewett et al 2007, Kohli 2005, Kohli &

Mather 2003, Thomas et al 2003, Mitchell 2003, Kidande & Amerena 2004, Kidane 2001).

In England local authorities children's services have a statutory duty under S.20 CA 1989 to safeguard and promote the welfare of children. The children to whom this duty applies are those who are in need" – S.17 (1) CA 1989.

It is argued that the mere fact that a child or young person is separated from their caregivers places them under this definition of a child 'in need' (Mitchell, 2003). Research suggests that it is the practice of most local authorities to 'accommodate' separated children under the age of 16 under S.20 CA 1989 with the majority of minors aged between 16-17 years being provided with services under the remit of S.17 (Cemlyn & Briskman, 2003). Although not specifically referred to in the Act, later guidance issued by the Department of Health (DoH Local Authority Circular 2003), indicates that this duty and related provisions also apply to unaccompanied asylum seeking children and young people. For the purposes of my dissertation, I will focus on those minors who are 'looked after' under S.20 CA 1989 and in foster care.

The DoH has provided a detailed framework for children's services role in assessing the needs of children and families known as the Framework for Assessment of Children In Need and their Families (DOH et al 2000). Non statutory guidance issued by the Department for Children, Schools and Families (2010) reiterates that local authorities are obliged to adopt the same approach in assessing the needs of an unaccompanied asylum seeking child as they use to assess other children in need. The Framework for Assessment of Children In Need and their Families (DOH et al 2000) is underpinned by an ecological perspective of an individual's human and social development and the areas to be considered when assessing the needs of a child or young person include:

- Their developmental needs including health, educational, emotional and behavioural needs, positive identity and social presentation, self care skills and family and social relationships

- The capacity of parent/s or caregiver/s to respond appropriately to those needs including providing basic care, safety, emotional warmth, and stability.
- The impact of wider family and environmental factors on the parents and child, such as housing, employment and family income (DoH et al 2000).

Whilst much of this information may be readily available for children who were born in the UK, this is not usually the case for separated children. Separated children are often the sole source of familial and other related information and how much, if any, of that information they choose to disclose has been the subject of much research (Chase 2009, Kohli et al 2007, Kohli, 2005).

Kohli suggests that there are many varied and complex reasons for 'silence' and selective disclosure which may include: an individual's desire for autonomy, acting on advice they have received from family members or others to remain silent, a fear talking about their lives and their experiences and 'silence' may also constitute a coping mechanism as a means of coping with the pain of loss and separation (2005). A small research study undertaken with 54 young people suggests that for many "...the predominant impetus for selective disclosure was a desire to retain a degree of agency as they navigated their way through a complex web of immigration, asylum, social care...systems..." (Chase 2009, 3). This undoubtedly poses challenges for social workers in seeking to assess their needs and in assessing their parents/caregivers capacity in their country of origin and the wider environmental factors which may have impacted on them whilst growing up. Often it is with time and as relationships are built between children and young people and their foster carers, social workers, teachers and others that this information can slowly be pieced together.

Health – Physical & Emotional Well-Being

Medical, optical and dental assessments are usually carried out within a short period after a separated child becomes looked after by the local authority. Sensitive areas such as mental health, advice and information pertaining to the use of alcohol, drugs, smoking and sexual health (which need to be dealt with in a culturally sensitive manner - Abunimah & Blower 2010), are usually carried out at a later stage.

In relation to emotional well-being Kohli & Mather argue that unaccompanied asylum seeking children arrive in the UK with a host of "...psychosocial needs associated with separation and resettlement..." (2003, 201) and suffering from 'cultural bereavement', a phrase originally coined by Esienbruch (Kohli & Mather 2003:205). Kohli & Mather highlight three main psychosocial barriers and challenges for separated children on arrival in the UK: adapting to learning the habits, rules and customs of their host country; owing to their experiences related to war separated children may be traumatised or haunted by 'ghosts from past'; and difficulties in navigating their way around the immigration and social care system.

Research highlights the fact that children and young people often experience symptoms such as disturbed sleep, feelings of isolation, depression, low self esteem, somatic symptoms, anxiety about their legal status and the effects of racism and bullying (Chase et al 2008, Derluyn & Broekaret 2008, Warwick et al 2006) and some young people report undergoing such emotional difficulties on a daily basis (Chase et al 2008).

In relation to mental health, studies exist indicating that many separated children manifest mental health problems and symptoms of Post Traumatic Stress Disorder (Hodges 2002). However, this is not always the case and in the absence of specific concerns, mental health needs are not usually assessed on arrival to the UK. A study by Hopkins & Hill (2010) highlights conflicting professional opinion as to whether access to mental health services should be available on arrival or when separated children have 'settled' into the UK.

The lack of professional consensus as to the merits for and against early intervention with respect to the timing of any mental health assessments, may result in separated children receiving different levels of service depending on the views of professionals within the areas where they live. Further to this, the wishes of the children and oung people in this regard is also an important factor. For instance,

it should be noted that interventions such as 'therapy' and

'counselling' may be 'alien' in concept for some separated children

who may have difficulties in comprehending what therapy entails or

they may feel stigmatised in using such services (Chase et al 2008).

A useful starting point may be the use of "...therapeutic care...rather

than therapy..." (Kohli & Mather 2003:206).

Promoting a positive sense of 'Identity'

An important means of promoting the general well-being of

separated children is in promoting a positive sense of their identity.

'Identity' is an extremely complex concept and is outside of the

scope of my dissertation to explore in any real depth. It can be

argued that there are certain aspects of one's 'identity' such as

physical attributes which are 'constant' and other aspects such as

culture, religion, sexuality etc which are more fluid. There are many

different perspectives on human and social development which are

relevant to the development of an individual's 'identity'.

4

Those who adopt an ecological perspective (based on Brofenbrenner's work 1979) of human development and social relationships would argue that one's identity is influenced by 'systems' such as the family ('microsystem'), local community ('exosystem') wider social and cultural factors ('macrosystem'), (Crawford & Walker 2007). Bowlby, (1979), and others who were influenced by this early theory of attachment, Bowlby, advocate that the 'quality' of an infant's attachment to their primary caregiver, (secure or insecure), results from the primary caregivers emotional attunement with and responses to the infant. This serves to provide the infant with a base upon which they develop a sense of themselves, others and a sense of the world and their place in the world, which they internalise. This internalisation serves to form an 'internal working model' within the child, influencing their emotional development, identity formation and social relationships throughout the lifespan.

Attachment theorists approach the subject of identity from a psychological perspective and argue that depending on whether an infant forms a secure or insecure attachment with their primary caregiver impacts on their ability to develop and sustain healthy attachments throughout their life.

Attachment theorists also argue that those with secure attachments are more likely to have positive self esteem and sense of self (Fonagy & Target 1997). An attachment between an infant and its caregiver is a something which occurs in all cultures, however, the interpretations ascribed to secure and insecure patterns of attachment are not accepted universally (Robinson 2007). An understanding of attachment theory is nonetheless extremely important in relation to fostering as it is argued that the quality of those previous influences an individual's ability to develop and sustain 'secondary' attachments with foster carers and others (including their peers).

Prior to becoming looked after, separated children have formed attachments to their primary parents or caregivers in their respective countries of origin. Separation from and the loss of these primary attachments has been shown to have a huge impact on a child's well-being, their health and their social relationships.

Human development and social relationships from a biological neuro-scientific perspective advocate that a child's cognitive and emotional development is sculpted in infancy by interactions with their primary caregivers and that these impact on the connections of the neural pathways in the developing brain (Sunderland 2006). This impact on the brain is not limited to infancy but is thought to be on-going throughout the lifespan.

Adolescence is a time of rapid growth spurt physically, cognitively, emotionally and also neurologically (Johnson et al 2009). Those who adopt a sociological and psychoanalytical perspective on human and social development, such as Erikson, view identity development as being influenced by the distinct life stages such as childhood, adolescence and right through to old age (Crawford & Walker 2007). The various different perspectives of human development, social relationships and the impact these may have on an individual's identity serve to illustrate that the concept of 'identity' is highly complex and is influenced by many factors.

Although the identities of individual separated children are already 'formed' to a greater or lesser extent, by the time they arrive in the UK, the process of adaptation and assimilation into the culture of the country they have fled to may also involve a certain level of disintegration of their former cultural identity (Maegusuku-Hewett et al 2007, Kohli & Mather 2003, Chase et al 2008). Research consistently highlights the importance of ethnicity, culture, language and religion in relation to positive identity formation and this is no less important for separated children.

In addition to meeting the needs of separated children and in providing a safe and supportive placement in which to live, there is no consensus as to whether these needs are best met in a placement with foster carers from a similar ethnic, cultural, linguistic and religious background. Kidane argues that "...the placement needs of choice for an unaccompanied refugee child is a placement

that reflects the child's ethnic, cultural and religious background..."
(2001, 13).

The shortage of foster carers nationally in the UK means that it is not always possible for separated children to be placed with carers who reflect their ethnic, cultural and religious backgrounds and often this means that many children are placed trans-culturally.

Research suggests that there are positive and negative aspects of children being placed in trans-cultural placements. In one study a young woman in a trans-cultural placement stated of her foster mother – "...she was a mother figure for me. We had a connection although we were from different cultures and different religions..." (Chase et al 2008, 69). However, a young man, having moved from a trans-cultural placement to a foster placement which reflected his ethnicity, culture and religion also spoke of the benefits – "...I get the chance not to forget my culture, I get the chance not to forget my religion, I get the chance not to forget my language..." (Chase et al 2008, 69).

A study by Luster et al (2008), relating to the experiences of Sudanese asylum seekers and refugees who had previously been in trans-cultural placements notes that cultural and language differences were often at the heart of placement disruptions. This study also highlights that other factors such as difficulties in accepting parental authority and conflicts relating to autonomy and trust were also highly relevant to placement disruptions. There will be those children and young people who wish to be in a placement that reflects their ethnicity, culture and religion whilst others may not, just as there will be those foster carers who are willing to receive trans-cultural placements and those who will not. Research articles which highlight some of the benefits of trans-cultural fostering, as well as the challenges has recently been undertaken by Brown et al (2009a, 2009b). The success or otherwise of placements often involves a combination of factors and at the heart of them is often the quality of relationship between the child and the foster carer and their families and the important aspect of 'cultural humility' (Brown 2009a) and compromise. A level of flexibility is also necessary in relation to taking into account the wishes of separated children in respect to fostering placements.

5

In order to maintain and promote links with the child's ethnicity and culture it is also necessary to include promoting contact with members of their family in their country of origin if this is possible and does not endanger the child or young person (Kidane 2001).

Spirituality and religion are important aspects of an individual's identity and have been identified as important by young people in numerous studies (Hill & Hopkins 2010, Jackson et al 2009, Chase et al 2008). Separated children should be given access to and support in order to practice their religious beliefs, attend places of worship, adhere to certain dietary requirements, and to observe certain festivals, if they so desire. Jackson et al explored the concept and importance of 'spirituality' via a small research study with around 188 young people aged between 14-17 in foster care in the US. The study suggests that "...spirituality is an important way to connect some youth to their culture..." (2009, 109). Another important aspect of promoting the welfare of separated children relates to their education.

Education

Whilst it should be noted that separated minors may or may not have had access to formal education in their countries of origin. The research highlights the importance of access to educational opportunities for separated children, if this is facilitated by support and understanding of diversity, as a factor which may facilitate their cultural integration into the host country, provide opportunities to make friendships and may impact on their emotional well-being (Hopkins & Hill 2010, Chase et al 2008, Kohli et al 2007, Berridge 2005, Kidane, 2001).

A study by Maegusuku-Hewett et al (2007) highlights that although children are often highly motivated to achieve and do well at school, school can sometimes be a place of conflict and bullying from peers. This highlights the need for support networks both inside and outside of the school in order to support separated children to achieve within the education system which also impacts on future aspirations and career prospects.

Access to Legal and Other Services

Several studies highlight the anxiety caused to separated children by the uncertainty over their immigration status and their future as an "overriding concern" (Chase et al 2008, 13). Research indicates that access to information about legal services and the immigration process are of the utmost importance to separated children and young people (Hopkins & Hill 2010, Crawley 2009, Chase et al 2008, Maegusuku-Hewett et al 2007, Kohli 2005, Kohli & Mather 2003). The Home Office recognises that the immigration process is not as child centred as it could be and has taken steps to endeavour to improve the service (HO 2007). Despite this endeavour however, the organisation, Refugee and Migrant Justice report that the service is still failing children and young people in many respects (2009). Relating to the immigration process and interviews conducted by the UKBA, a small sample of young people who shared their experiences state feeling that "...what they have to say about their experiences is often not listened to, let alone heard or understood..." (Crawley, 2009, 167).

Overall, research findings suggest that both practical and emotional support needs to be given to separated children not just from the outset but throughout the process of accessing immigration and other services.

Various studies highlight the importance of providing separated children with access to informal advocacy services and tracing services such as the Red Cross, (Hopkins & Hill 2010, Kidane 2001). Once the kinds of services on offer have been explained to young people, it is up to them to make a decision of whether to avail themselves of such services. In regards to promoting contact between separated children and their family and friends who are in their country of origin or elsewhere this needs to be facilitated sensitively and safely so as not to endanger the children, young people themselves and/or others.

Promoting a child or young person's positive sense of identity also serves to promote their use of resilience and coping strategies.

Coping Strategies and Resilience

At the outset I would like to acknowledge that I recognise that there is no agreed definition as to what constitutes 'resilience', nor is there agreement as to "...what factors and processes promote or result in resilience..." (Maegusuku-Hewett et al, 2007, 311). When using the term 'resilience' I have adopted a definition used by Gilligan (2004:93) "... a dynamic process encompassing positive adaptation within the context of severe adversity..." because it conveys the sense of resilience as being more than an inner personal quality, but as an ongoing, adaptive process.

Maegusuku-Hewett et al (2007) note that research studies often fail to take into account the child and young person's understanding of resilience and the factors that they themselves attribute to helping them cope. In a study undertaken by Maegusuku-Hewett et al, the researchers took note of the factors young people identified as mechanisms that young people used regularly to help them cope.

Young people identified the following factors: having an optimistic outlook on life; segregation from or integration with the host culture; the development of a positive, social identity and being patient.

Similar themes were identified in other research studies where young people identified various challenges they faced and their coping strategies including the following: adapting to life in the UK by learning to speak English, having a optimistic outlook on life and remaining hopeful, using distraction and keeping themselves busy as a means of not dwelling on sad thoughts and feelings and access to and participation in leisure activities (Ni Raghallaigh & Gilligan 2010, Chase et al 2008, Kohli 2007).

Kohli & Mather suggest that: therapeutic care (not necessarily therapy), a regeneration of a sense of belonging, the development of personal autonomy and control, development of skills and participation in activities, development of security and practical support are factors that enhance the promotion of psychosocial well-being and coping strategies of unaccompanied asylum seeking young people (2003). Ni Raghallaigh & Gilligan's findings suggest, in the majority of cases, that religion was at the heart of the coping strategies that young people identified as helpful (2009).

The fundamental role of spirituality and religion in the development of coping strategies and resilience was not something I had expected to see from the research, however it emerged as such a strong theme that it would have been unethical of me to ignore or seek to exclude its significance. In a small empirical research study with around 188 young people aged between 14-17 in foster care in the US, Jackson et al (2009) explored the concept and importance of 'spirituality' as a coping mechanism.

Notwithstanding the difficulties in defining the concept of spirituality that was not too restrictive nor linked spirituality to any specific religion, Jackson et al suggest that spirituality is an important aspect of culture but also acts as a means of both internal and external support in the face of grief and loss. Studies undertaken in the UK also highlight the importance of religion in the lives of separated children (Hopkins & Hill 2010, Ni Raghallaigh & Gilligan 2009, Chase et al 2008).

In view of research findings it would seem that access to and support to practice their religious beliefs is of fundamental importance to many separated children and should be facilitated by foster carers where required.

Having considered the research findings in relation to separated children, I will now present the research findings in respect of the effectiveness of foster carers' training.

RESEARCH FINDINGS

Foster Carers' Training

In England foster carers are governed by the Fostering Services Regulations 2002. It is general practice that foster carers undergo pre-approval training as part of their fostering assessment. One of the most widely used training programmes for foster carers in preparation to foster is 'The Skills to Foster' course published by Fostering Network (Fostering Network 2009).

This publication was designed as a training manual/workbook and does not constitute 'research' in a formal, academic sense. The training course consists of themes which have been the subject of extensive research, some of which have been incorporated into the training.

'The Skills to Foster' course has been designed to be run over a 3 day period and it covers six modules which are as follows: 'What do foster carers do?' 'Identity and life chances', 'Working with others', 'Understanding children in foster care', 'Safer caring' and 'Transitions'.

'The Skills to Foster' course outlines the role and responsibilities of foster carers and the laws, regulations and minimum standards which govern the fostering role. The course makes use of individual and group work exercises which allow potential foster carers opportunities to reflect on who they 'are' as individuals, their heritage, and culture. It allows for discussions relating to carers' experiences of parenting and being parented and how this may impact on the care they offer to looked after children. For those with families, the course discusses the importance of involving their families in their decision whether or not to foster.

'The Skills to Foster' course highlights topics such as reasons why children and young people become looked after and the importance of safeguarding and promoting their welfare. It covers the importance of anti-discriminatory practice and respecting diversity in relation to a child or young person's ethnicity, culture, language and religious beliefs, maintaining links to their heritage and contact with their family and other significant people.

'The Skills to Foster' course incorporates research shown to be effective in relation to effective parenting and in promoting security of attachment in foster children. 'The Secure Base Star', which consists of five fundamental aspects of parenting, was originally identified by Ainsworth et al and developed by Schofield and Beck

(Schofield 2010). The five elements of 'The Secure Base Star'

framework are as follows: the availability of foster carers helping

children to trust, sensitivity in helping children manage their feelings

and behaviour, acceptance of foster children and helping to build

their self esteem, cooperation in the sense of helping children to

develop a sense of efficacy and family membership and helping

children to feel they belong to the family (Schofield, 2010).

'The Skills to Foster' course offers an excellent introduction to

fostering, however, its limitations with respect to those foster carers

considering fostering unaccompanied asylum seekers is

acknowledged by Fostering Network who advise that carers should

receive "...additional support and information" from their fostering

service (Fostering Network 2009, Module 2, 11). The course

includes a short section at the end of 'Identity and life chances'

(Module 2), which outlines possible previous experiences of

separated children and possible reasons for migration from their

country of origin. It also outlines the support and care separated children will need from their foster carers in adapting to their new lives in the UK and in navigating the legal immigration process.

The course briefly examines attachment theory and the importance of recognising the impact that separation and loss of those primary attachments may have upon children and young people. In looking at this section of the training publication, I recalled previously reading a resource which challenged common perspectives on the interpretations commonly ascribed to different attachment patterns termed as 'secure' (ideal) or 'insecure' (somewhat deficient). In her book entitled 'Cross-cultural child development for social workers', Robinson argues that not all cultures view attachment patterns in the same light (2007) and that social workers could unwittingly mis-interpret patterns of attachment.

In light of this argument and in the interests of respect for diversity, perhaps a note of caution should be sounded and a measure of cultural sensitivity applied when interpreting different styles of attachment for children from different cultures.

'Fostering Unaccompanied Asylum Seeking and Refugee Children –
A Training Course for Foster Carers' (Kidane & Amerena 2004) is a
post approval training course designed by BAAF for foster carers
caring for or considering caring for children and young people who
have migrated from their country of origin. Although this publication
is designed as a training course and not as 'research', the course
consists of themes which have been the subject of extensive
research. The course includes group and individual exercises which
allows for opportunities for foster carers to reflect on their own life
and parenting experiences and how they can use this insight gained
into themselves and their families to parent separated children.

'Fostering Unaccompanied Asylum Seeking and Refugee
Children...' outlines possible reasons for migration, and experiences
that some may have faced pre-flight and during migration. The
course explores the needs of unaccompanied asylum seeking and
refugee children, and explores the potential impact of being
separated from their families. It also highlights some of the

behaviours which may be indicative of trauma and distress and the potential side effects of secondary trauma to those caring for separated children.

Although Fox is not writing from the perspective of a foster carer when she writes that "...in caring for the carers we are also serving the needs of the refugees themselves..." (Fox 2010, 190), her comments could equally have a wider application to carers in different contexts. I feel that secondary trauma is an issue that should be addressed in pre and post approval training for foster carers. 'Fostering Unaccompanied Asylum Seeking Children and Refugees – A Training Course for Foster Carers' (Kidane & Amerena 2004) also explores factors that may reduce or strengthen resilience and how foster carers can endeavour to promote resilience. The importance of foster carers' supporting separated children through the immigration process, catering for their practical needs and preparing young people for independent living, are also topics included in the course.

The stated purpose of both Fostering Network and BAAF's training courses are to prepare foster carers for the role of fostering. Alongside this primary purpose, the respective courses are also designed to help potential carers to decide whether or not they wish to foster and the case of BAAF's course, whether they wish to foster unaccompanied asylum seeking children and refugees. Puddy & Jackson's respective research project involved evaluating the effectiveness of the MAPP/GPS training course for foster carers (2003).

Puddy & Jackson argue that where training primarily focuses on making a decision of whether to become foster carers and not on important areas such as "...basic child management techniques, this creates a false expectation for foster parents. Without proper training in communication, discipline strategies... those receiving MAPP/GPS training are ill-prepared to deal with the real challenges of foster children" (2003, 1006). Although I recognise that Puddy & Jackson's criticisms were in respect of this particular course (MAPP/GPS), this duality of purpose, as emphasised in the UK training courses, may act as a 'sieve' with regards to those who are committed to fostering, which could be seen in a positive light.

BAAF, Fostering Network and other organisations offer a number of courses related to fostering separated children. To the best of my knowledge there have not been any independent research studies evaluating the effectiveness of such courses.

A review of research highlights different avenues of training such as specialist training, group work training among foster carers, individual training with foster carers within their own homes, joint training of foster carers with social workers and the informal training of foster carers by their foster children. Research also highlights factors that may impact on foster carer's acquisition of knowledge and skills through training and whether the training undertaken improves their practice and impacts on improved outcomes for foster children.

Avenues of Training & Contributory Factors Influencing their Effectiveness

Specialist Training

Luster et al's study undertaken in the US with Sudanese young people speaking about their experiences of foster care retrospectively, argue that "...all foster parents of refugee youth should be offered more specialised training that deals with the unique combination of factors affecting parent-child relationships, cultural differences, adolescence and the effects of trauma..." (2009,394).

A Consultation Paper by the Home Office (2007) includes a reference to a proposal to create "specialist foster parents for unaccompanied asylum seeking children" (2007, 14). This proposal was not implemented by the former Labour Government and is unlikely to be pursued by the former Coalition Government. The fact that such a proposal may have been considered or put forward, ndicates the importance of additional training for foster carers aring for separated children has been recognised. A study by Warwick et al based in Huddersfield found that social workers felt eskilled and inadequate "...when confronted with the enormity of ne life experiences and traumas experienced by asylum seekers..." 2006, 131). A study by Brown et al (2009b) suggests that where oster carers feel 'inadequacy' that training may go some way to mproving their levels of confidence.

Separated children come from various ethnic and cultural ackgrounds. Brown et al (2009a) argue that the most effective way o "promote cultural continuity in fostering is to promote cultural natching in placements' (2009a, 283), a point previously made by Kidane (2001).

The shortage of foster carers, globally and nationally (Colton et al 2008) includes a shortage of foster carers from black and minority ethnic groups. Therefore many children and young people are nevitably placed in trans-cultural foster placements. A study by

Brown et al (2009a, 2009b) suggests that foster carers' confidence in caring for children and young people from different ethnicities and cultures is enhanced when they receive related training. This study dealt with trans-cultural fostering of Aboriginal refugees by Canadian foster carers. The foster carers' received training that included developing self awareness of their own prejudices and an appreciation and valuing of diversity of others. What struck me was the acknowledgement by the foster carers in this particular study of the importance of developing "cultural humility" (2009a, 282), which involves "changing one's perspective to view other cultures as equally valid to one's own..." (2009a, 282).

The foster carers concerned spoke about how challenging they found making such adjustments. Nevertheless, they preserved and later were able to report how they felt they had benefited from fostering children and young people from different backgrounds to themselves.

Pre and post-approval fostering courses run by Fostering Network and BAAF deal with issues relating to diversity training. At the assessment stage, foster carers are assessed on issues relating to diversity and their receptivity to diversity, interests in learning about other cultures and their willingness to support a looked after child in

this respect. Whilst many of the issues common to the general population of looked after children are also shared by separated children, foster carers may benefit from acquiring additional information which specifically address the unique situation of separated children.

Research findings suggest that foster carers value sharing experiences and learning from other foster carers, social workers and foster children.

Learning from others

Allen & Vostanis note that foster carers "...valued hearing and learning from the experiences and views of other carers..." (2005,

76). This theme is highlighted by several other studies (Warman et al 2006, Allen & Vostanis 2005, Golding & Picken 2004). Allen & Vostanis state that based on the comments given by foster carers with respect to the training the implication was that they felt a sense of "...commonality and recognition that other carers are in the same position..." (2005, 76). Foster carers are also more likely to give of themselves and share their fostering experiences if their training takes place in an atmosphere which is conducive to learning, and one which encourages trust and openness (Warman et al 2006). Hill-Tout et al note that it is important that "...individuals feel safe and comfortable in the group environment..." (2003, 51). These factors are important because of the sensitive and confidential information which is shared in such forums.

Titterington highlights the benefits of joint training between social workers and foster carers (1990). Titterington refers to a 'team approach' to training where the social workers bring a theoretical perspective and case experience to training and the foster carers bring their skills and knowledge in terms of practical experience.

The 'team' approach to fostering was found to be beneficial by social workers in a study by Allen & Vostanis (2005), where the researchers examined the issue of joint training between foster carers and social workers in relation to a course on attachment theory and the impact of trauma on a developing child. The participants of the study reported that one of the advantages of joint training was that foster carers had accessible support from their supervising social workers during the course and after course completion.

Individual versus Groupwork Training

Having discussed some of the advantages of learning from other foster carers and joint training with social workers, a study by Hampson (1983) set out to measure the effectiveness of a parent training programme for foster carers by comparing "...whether an individualised training approach would result in increased learning, motivation and satisfaction for foster parents when compared with those engaged in group training experience?" (Hampson 1983, 193).

A total of 29 foster carers from 18 families were involved in the study, half of whom were trained in groups with the remaining foster carers were trained individually in their homes over an 11 week period. Interestingly, Hampson et al's findings reveal that there was little difference between the two groups, with both groups having reported an increase in their knowledge of parenting and improvements in the child's behaviour as a result of putting into practice the behavioural techniques they had learnt.

An interesting 'by-product' of the individual training conducted within the foster carer's home that I noted was that it served to "increase the involvement of foster fathers in the foster child-rearing area" (Hampson et al 1983, 200). The theme of how to encourage greater involvement of male carers in fostering and training is an interesting theme, however, time constraints and the scope of my dissertation prevent me from exploring this issue further. In terms of comparing individual training and group training, Hampson et al acknowledge that one of the disadvantages of individual training is that it is not cost effective.

With regards to the advantages offered by training groups, Golding & Picken argue that group work is an "efficient use of limited resources" and it allows organisers to "...provide support to a number of carers at the same time while also giving them opportunities to learn and support one another" (2004,34). Foster carers cited the support that they received from other carers had a stabilising effect on their placement thus contributing to positive outcomes for those children and young people whose placement may have been at risk from disruption (Golding & Picken 2004, Hampson et al 1983). For this reason, Golding & Picken view group work as a positive form of intervention. However, the advantages of group work, Golding & Picken acknowledge that there are challenges for foster carers in terms of time and commitment (2004). In weighing up the advantages and disadvantages of both individual and group work training, research evidence suggests that both avenues of training are useful.

Informal training by foster children

7

At the outset of my research project, when I was considering the issue of training for foster carers, I inadvertently overlooked a potentially rich source of foster carer training, namely the training by the children and young people they foster. In a research study by Brown et al (2009a, 2009b), the foster carers acknowledged the contribution made by their foster children in their learning experiences of and informal training in matters relating to the children's heritage, identity and culture. Several of the foster parents described their foster children as their "...teachers and leaders of change..." (2009a, 283). This is an informal avenue of training that I had originally overlooked. Although the authors of this research acknowledge that their findings are not representative of foster carers universally, it could be argued that the interchange of learning between foster carers and their foster children is probably a common phenomenon which should be celebrated and encouraged.

Research findings suggest that effective avenues of training foster carers can also be linked to factors relating to the approach taken to learning, the demographic profile of foster carers and trainers and the duration of training and the intervals between sessions.

Active Approach to Learning

Warman et al's (2006) findings suggest that an active approach to learning is effective because it "...emphasises trying out ideas and skills – 'doing it' rather than simply 'talking' or 'thinking' about it..." (2006, 21). The researchers note that "in using and experiencing these skills that the deepest and most persuasive learning occurs" (2006, 22). Active learning was recognised as important over 20 years previously in a study by Guerney & Wolfgang who felt that experiential skills training "should be emphasised in addition to information and discussion" (1981, 34). In terms of the style of training courses Hampson et al's (1983) findings suggest that an element of reflective training (open communication between foster carers and looked after children through awareness, acceptance and understanding), and behavioural training (principles relating to behaviour modification) are most effective.

Reflective training is a feature in both 'The Skills to Foster' and the 'Fostering Unaccompanied Asylum Seekers and Refugee Children – A Training Course for Foster Carers'. Both reflective and behavioural training forms the basis of the 'Fostering Changes' course designed for the London Borough of Southwark for its fostering and adoption services.

Demographic Profile of foster carers and course trainers

Findings from a study by Puddy & Jackson (2003) suggest that the MAPP/GPS training course was unsuccessful in preparing potential foster carers for the fostering role. The authors of the research suggest that this may have related to the demographic profile of the sample group (including education status and learning abilities) and the potential impact these may have had on their level of acquisition of parenting knowledge and skills. This raises an important issue with regards to training courses generally.

Are training courses designed and delivered with different levels of expertise and cognitive abilities in mind? Do they take into account possible barriers to learning such as learning difficulties, dyslexia and previous experiences of training? (Warman et al 2006). Does the training take into account the characteristics of a group and the impact of favourable or unfavourable group dynamics? These are factors which may potentially negatively impact on foster carers' acquisition of knowledge and skills, if not identified and addressed.

In contrast to the study by Puddy & Jackson (2003), Allen & Vostanis noted that the foster carers in their sample group were described as "very experienced, resourceful and skilled..." (2005, 78). For me, this raises questions which relate to the representativeness of sample groups and their demographic characteristics in relation to the general population of foster carers? It also raises the 'thorny' issue of, what is the best 'level' at which to pitch training? Should training be pitched at specific levels of knowledge and abilities or should it be pitched at a 'basic' level and then adjusted accordingly? Often fostering agencies adopt a 'one size fits all' approach to training, which may suit some but not all. Puddy & Jackson (2003) also note the potential impact of a trainer's personal characteristics and their skill and style of delivery can have on skills acquisition. Warman et al note that the ability of a trainer is important because it enables them to draw out the "...inherent strengths and abilities of members of the group, to enable them to learn with and through each other..." (2006, 21).

Course Timings

Research suggests that training course duration and the length of intervals between each training session contribute towards the success of training because it provides foster carers with "...opportunities to practice what they have learnt within the programme and in between sessions..." (Macdonald & Turner 2005, 1279), an important factor noted in other studies (Warman et al 2006, Allen & Vostanis 2005, Golden & Picken 2004, Hill-Tout et al 2003).

There is no consensus as to at what stage during a foster carer's career they would most benefit from 'specialist' training. A study by Allen & Vostanis, examined the effectiveness of foster carers and ocial workers' joint training in attachment theory and the impact of

rauma on a developing child.

Social workers attending this joint training expressed the following

views:

- Training should be part of the pre-approval assessment

  process,
- Training should take place shortly after approval,
- Training should be offered once foster carers had some

  experience of the fostering role and therefore could relate to

  the material.

nterestingly, the foster carers undertaking the course were of the

opinion that those carers who would benefit most from the specialist

training would be those who had "...experience of caring for children

... with a history of abuse and trauma to relate to the material

discussed..." (2005, 77). It is not surprising that there is a lack of

consensus in views between those carrying out the fostering role

and those supporting them. However, perhaps a way forward would

be for a brief introduction to caring for separated children to form part of the pre-approval introductory courses, such as is already the case in Fostering Network's 'The Skills to Foster'. Once a foster carer has been approved and has some experience of fostering and expresses an interest in caring for separated children, additional courses such as the one offered by BAAF can then be accessed.

Having considered various themes highlighted by research in relation to foster carers', I will now present the findings as to whether training is effective in improving foster carer practice and outcomes for the children fostered.

Mixed Messages from Research Findings

In 2005 the former Labour Government's commissioned a large scale overview of fostering entitled 'Fostering Now: Messages from research', found that despite having some merits, "...training for carers had no simple, direct link with improved child outcomes..." (Berridge, 2005, 8). These findings, as disappointing as they appear, seem to be echoed in the majority of the research studies in relation to pre and post approval training even where foster carers have positively evaluated the training (Schofield 2010, Allen &

Vostanis 2005, Golding & Picken 2005, Macdonald & Turner 2005, Hill-Tout et al 2003, and Minis et al 2001, Fees et al 1988, Hampson 1983) with few noticeable exceptions (Warman et al 2006, Golding & Picken 2005, Guerney & Wolfgang 1981).

Prior to presenting the research findings, it is important to acknowledge the challenges involved in trying to measure outcomes in relation to training courses. Measuring outcomes often involves a high level of subjectivity on the part of those carrying out such measurements (Golding & Picken 2004). In analysing the research findings, certain questions arise such as:

- Are evaluations simply measuring foster carer's or social workers perceptions of outcomes?
- Should foster children's views of outcomes be measured?
- How useful are evaluations and how soon after completion of training should outcomes be measured?

In relation to the last issue, in a study by Fees et al (1998), the researchers delayed their evaluation of pre-approval foster care training until 1 year after completion of the course. The reason for doing so was that it was felt to be a more appropriate time to test the effectiveness of the training because it would take place "...after participants had had an opportunity to apply the information learned and to recognise the issues for which training did or did not adequately cover or prepare them..." (Fees et al 1998, 351). Despite the delayed evaluation of the course, Fees et al's findings suggest that even though the foster carers expressed satisfaction with the training they had received, there was little evidence to show that it had impacted on their direct practice, nor had it impacted on improved outcomes for the foster children, as it had been hoped.

Minis et al (2001) conducted a randomised control trial with fostering families undertaking mental health training. Minis et al findings were that although the foster carers highly rated the training, there was little evidence to suggest that it had had positive outcomes in terms of the emotional behavioural functioning of the children and young people looked after. Puddy & Jackson's findings suggest that, in their particular study, the MAPP/GPS training course curriculum "...appears to be less than effective in preparing parents for the challenging role of being a foster parent..." (2003, 1004). A study by Hill-Tout et al (2003) examined the impact of a 3 day training course (delivered over a period of 3 weeks) focusing on behavioural management techniques.

As has been noted in previous studies, although the training course was positively evaluated by foster carers, it seemed to have limited impact on their fostering capacity or on the behaviour of the children fostered. Macdonald & Turner's study involved conducting a randomised control trial with groups of foster carers (117 participants in all) in order to "...find out whether training foster carers in methods designed to help people better manage challenging behaviour would have benefits for looked after children and foster carers..." (2005, 1267).

The findings of this study suggest that despite the foster carers expressing satisfaction with the training, this did not correlate with their applying the cognitive-behavioural management techniques demonstrated in the course, nor did training impact on the behavioural issues experienced by the children and young people looked after. In analysing the research findings, it would appear that there were a number of contributory factors which may have impacted on foster carers' acquisition of knowledge and skills and outcomes for those they foster which I will briefly comment on. Contributory factors include:

- The demographic profile of foster carers, such as educational status, learning abilities, learning difficulties, personal and environmental concerns of foster carers (Hill-Tout 2003, Puddy & Jackson 2003). Puddy & Jackson express the view that this may have had a negative impact on the lack of positive outcomes with respect to those potential foster carers attending the MAPP/GPS course. Warman et al (2006) note the importance of identifying and addressing potential barriers to learning.
- The profile of course trainers, their expertise and their style of delivering the training (Hill-Tout et al 2003, Guerney &

Wolfgang 1981). In respect of course trainers, Guerney & Wolfgang pose the question "...Is a program effective only in the hands of certain personality types?" In the majority of instances researchers try to minimise the impact of this variable to ensure consistency of delivery.

- A 'one size fits all approach' is not an effective form of training for everyone (Hill-Tout et al 2003), although it is often the most practical, the most cost effective and the most widely used method of training,

- The length of a training course and the intervals between each training session has been noted to be significant in terms of outcomes. However time constraints and resources will inevitably be a deciding factor for most fostering agencies.

Macdonald & Turner note the "...lack of available support within the agencies to help foster carers implement newly acquired skills..." as possibly being a significant contributor in the disappointing results of their study (2005, 1278). This implies that whilst fostering agencies are prepared to invest in training for foster carers, more attention is needed with regards to post training support.

Warman et al (2006) and Guerney & Wolfgang (1981) provide examples of effective training for foster carers with positive results in terms of improving foster carers' practice and outcomes for the children and young people they foster. The Warman et al study evaluated an in-house training course designed for the London Borough of Southwark's fostering and adoption services entitled 'Fostering Changes'. The focus of 'Fostering Changes' was to promote "...positive relationships between carers and the children...as well as developing the carers' abilities to manage behavioural problems..." (2006, 20). Warman et al's findings suggest that the training was successful in meeting its purpose of influencing the foster carers' practice and in producing better outcomes for the foster children.

The second study involved a long range evaluation of an in-house skills training programme for foster carers undertaken in the US by

Guerney & Wolfgang (1981). In summary, the findings suggest that the training programme was effective because it impacted positively on foster carers' attitudes towards the children fostered, the foster parents were able to use their acquired knowledge and skills to further promote the child and parent relationship and the foster carers felt able to respond more positively to behaviour management. Guerney & Wolfgang claim successful results were replicated time and again using different groups of foster carers and different trainers.

When it came to analysing what factors may have contributed to the successful outcomes of the foster carers' training in those two research studies, several factors emerge:

- The 'Fostering Changes' programme was based on a parenting programme format that has been proven to be highly successful. This format includes: a mixture between reflective training and behaviour modification training (Hampson et al 2003), the course is set over a number of weeks which allows the foster carers the opportunity to put into practice some of the skills and knowledge they are acquiring (Warman et al 2006, Allen & Vostanis 2005, Macdonald & Turner 2005, Golding & Picken 2004, Hill-Tout et al 2003),

- The course involves group work and shared learning experiences (Berridge 2006, Warman et al 2006, Allen & Vostanis 2005, Golding & Picken 2004).

- An active approach to learning was adopted in both studies by Warman et al (2006) and Guerney & Wolfgang (1981),

- In the study by Warman et al (2006), attention was paid to establishing an environment which the foster carers felt was open and one in which they felt 'safe'.

- In the study by Warman et al (2006), potential barriers to learning such as learning difficulties and or previous negative experiences of learning were identified and addressed,

- Trainers are viewed not as experts but as facilitators in the training.

Whilst not wishing to dispute the findings of Guerney & Wolfgang (1981), the findings should be treated with a degree of caution bearing in mind that Guerney was both author of the research and also responsible for developing the training programme which was being evaluated by the research study. These findings demonstrate that effective training programmes are those which impact positively on foster carers' practice and also produce positive outcomes for the children fostered.

Having completed the summary of the research findings in relation to effective training for foster carers, I will now present the conclusion to my research project.

CONCLUSION

In reviewing the research related to effective avenues of foster carers' training, as a former foster carer and social work student, I am somewhat disappointed by the research findings. Overall, the findings strongly suggest that foster carers' training does not necessarily result in improved outcomes in terms of improved foster carers' practice nor in improved outcomes for the children they foster, despite positive evaluation of the training by foster carers.

The studies by Warman et al (2006) and Guerney & Wolfgang (1981) provide examples of where foster carers' training has been effective in both areas. In spite of my personal disappointment, the research findings are useful however, in identifying contributory factors which may impact positively or negatively on the effectiveness of foster carers' training.

The findings contain information which may assist local authorities and fostering services in incorporating those positive aspects identified by the research into their future training models. These positive aspects of training include:

- Active learning
- Learning alongside others – (shared learning)
- Potential barriers to learning being identified and addressed

- Intervals between training sessions to allow for reflection and practice of skills and knowledge gained
- Good training facilitators
- An environment which is conducive to learning and sharing
- Commitment from foster carers and trainers
- Post training support

At the outset of my research project my expectations were that the findings would demonstrate, that training is, on the whole, an effective means of preparing foster carers for the challenges of fostering, (although none of the research studies related specifically to foster carers' training in caring for separated children). I had also assumed that if the foster carers had made the commitment to attend and participate in training then this would result in carers adapting their fostering practice in light of what they had learnt. Additionally, I had also erroneously assumed that if foster carers' training impacted positively on their practice this would have a positive impact (more often than not) on the children they fostered.

The findings of my research project have challenged and refuted these assumptions. Previously, I had erroneously equated positive evaluation of foster carers' training with positive outcomes, however research strongly demonstrates otherwise (Allen & Vostanis 2005, Golding & Picken 2005, Macdonald & Turner 2005, Hill-Tout et al 2003, Minis et al 2001, Fees et al 1988). Despite this, it was encouraging to note that even in those instances where training was ineffective in improving outcomes for foster carers and children, the positive evaluation of training by the foster carers, implies that training is useful.

Research has consistently highlighted that separated children have additional and unique needs arising from their experiences of separation from their parents, migration and resettlement and also their immigration status. Research has reaffirmed my perspective that the role of a foster carer is necessary despite its challenges. For this reason, the role of social workers in providing good support for foster carers and the children and young people they foster is of vital importance. I have come to appreciate that in terms of improving outcomes for looked after children including separated children, foster carers are only part of the solution. Other agencies and professionals such as social workers, teachers, schools, colleges, health providers and so on, also need to play an active role.

The research project was undertaken with a simplistic and somewhat idealistic perspective of what training encompassed and what it could accomplish. At that stage I had failed to consider that other factors such as the profile of foster carers, trainers, the training environment, the length of training and the intervals between each session and so on, could impact on the effectiveness of training.

At the outset of the project, I was not aware of the variety of training avenues available and had completely overlooked the matter of foster parents receiving training by the children and young people they foster (Brown et al 2009a, 2009b). In spite of my idealistic expectations on what foster carers' training would accomplish, I am pleased that I had made a conscious effort, throughout the research project, to remain open-minded as to what the research finding may reveal. In the end, the assumptions that I had started out with turned out to be incorrect and without foundation, which I accept.

Towards the end of my research project, I started to think about how I would undertake this project where I would do it again with the hindsight that I have gained. I compiled a list of things that I would do again and the things I would change.

One of the most significant things that I would change, relates to not considering the importance of 'research and ethics' at the outset of my project. I feel that my impulsiveness and enthusiasm to delve into the subject overshadowed my thought processes and clouded my judgement. In hindsight I wish that I had given this area greater prominence at the beginning of the project. I feel that had I done so, I may have selected other research studies, which may have reduced any 'researcher bias' I may have had. However, I do accept that this may not have impacted on the result of the research findings. If there had been more time available, I would have liked to have conducted other database searches and explored the area of on-line training for foster carers, an aspect of training that I have omitted to consider in my research project.

In terms of the things that I would do all over again, I would have chosen the same subject matter which held my interest throughout the project and continues to inspire me. I feel that some of what I have learnt about fostering and caring for separated children will be useful throughout my therapeutic work.

For instance, I have learnt that it is a personal strength and not a sign of weakness to admit when having made incorrect assumptions and to use that experience to challenge other personal and professional assumptions. In social work working alongside service users, some of whom are highly vulnerable, I have learnt that by staying in a personal comfort zone and not challenging myself on a regular basis could have a detrimental impact for myself professionally and personally, for the service user and for the social work profession. I have also come to appreciate the importance of social work research as a means of developing and disseminating knowledge and good practice.

Highly developed organisational skills proved to be invaluable asset from the outset of the project. I found that compiling a list of references which I added and subtracted from articles was a useful tool in terms of analysing the type of articles, the volume of articles I had been reading and whether they related to foster carers' training and/or separated children.

If I had to start the research project over again, I would revise and re-use the 4 page questionnaire format that I devised, as a means of recording certain themes in each article I read, such as: research themes; good or poor research practices; effective or ineffective training methods; needs and resilience of separated children and so on.

Here is a brief summary of the findings of my research project and

its implications for social work practice:

- Foster carers' training is costly in terms of financial resources
  and time commitment from foster carers, social workers and
  trainers. In order to get the most out of training and to
  maximise its effectiveness, lessons from research findings
  should be considered by local authorities and other fostering
  agencies commissioning training;

- There are various avenues of foster carers' training. Perhaps
  more emphasis needs to be applied to thinking of ways in
  which to use these avenues more creatively and effectively –
  for example, structuring foster carer support groups in such a
  way so that they offer an element of support as well as an
  element of training in specific areas of interest. This would
  involve social workers often facilitating such groups to
  organise training themes and agendas as identified by the
  department and or the foster carers themselves. Is time given
  to thinking about how both support and training can be
  incorporated into supervision sessions between a foster carer

and their supervising social worker? Should joint training between foster carers and social workers be commissioned (Allen & Vostanis 2005, Titterington 1990) related to separated children? Is it possible to do more to incorporate the perspectives of foster children within training, as is already the case with both Fostering Network (2009) and BAAF 's(2006) training courses?

- In terms of providing effective foster carer training, local authorities and other fostering services may like to consider investing more in post training support to "...help foster carers implement newly acquired skills..." (Macdonald & Turner 2005, 1278), so as to make the most effective use of their investment in training;

- Research has strongly demonstrated that an area which has been identified as important by separated children and young people is in the matter of religion and spirituality. In the interests of respecting diversity and promoting looked after childrens' well-being, this is a topic which is not often the subject of foster carers' training, or social workers' training but in the light of research findings is something that may need to be considered in the future.

In undertaking this research project, one of the things that became evident early on, was that "...relatively little research exists that explores the fostering of unaccompanied children either from their own perspective or from that of the foster carers supporting them..." (HEK 2007, 109). The significance of this is that I have had to draw conclusions from findings on research of foster carers' training which was not necessarily related to caring for separated children.

A joint research undertaken by the University of York and the University of Bedfordshire, exploring the issue raised above, had not been completed when I was undertaking the research project. The researchers noted that they were confident that they would be able to utilise their findings in order to "...prepare practice guidance to support the development of effective fostering policies and practice within unaccompanied children..." (2009-20011). The researchers were hopeful that the findings of this study would offer a further contribution to the understanding of the fostering role and the experiences of foster carers caring for separated children and the fostering experiences of separated children.

From the perspective of a former therapeutic foster carer and as a therapeutic support worker, who has worked alongside foster carers caring for separated children and young people, the research project has re-affirmed that the role of a foster carer can be extremely challenging yet rewarding.

Currently there is a national shortage of available foster carers, particularly from ethnic minorities. A study undertaken by Hutchinson suggests that in order to provide an effective fostering service that local authorities and other fostering agencies need to "...develop a tailored approach to training foster carers by assessing the needs of the looked after children in their locality..." (2003, 12).

Despite the challenges involved in undertaking such a task, a service which is tailored may offer benefits both to foster children and carers, as well as being an efficient use of limited resources. Many local authorities, however, place separated children with foster carers who live outside of the borough and thus separated children may suffer disadvantage under such a scheme.

During the time that I have spent in undertaking my research project I have noted a number of topics which might be addressed in future research. These topics include:

- An independent evaluation of the effectiveness of specialist training courses for foster carers caring for separated children
- The availability, accessibility and effectiveness of on-line training for foster carers
- Attachment styles of separated children and how these impact on cross cultural fostering.

Separated children who are looked after by local authorities have specific needs and develop resilience borne out of their unique circumstances. It is therefore important for social workers of separated children and young people and foster carers to understand that "...they are ...not extraordinary children, but children in extraordinary circumstances..." (Kohli 2008, 210).

Bibliography

Abunimah, A. & Blower, S. (2010). 'The Circumstances and Needs of Separated Children Seeking Asylum in Ireland', Child Care in Practice, 16, (2), 129-146.

Allen, J. & Vostanis, P. (2005). 'The impact of abuse and trauma on the developing child. An evaluation of a training programme for foster carers and supervising social workers', Adoption & Fostering, 29, (3), 68-81.

Berridge, D. (2005). 'Fostering Now: Messages from research – a summary', Adoption & Fostering, 29, (4), 6-8.

Bhabha, J. & Finch N. (2006). Seeking Asylum Alone.

ttp://www.irr.org.uk/pdf2/SAA_UK.pdf

Accessed: 19/07/10]

Bhabha, J. (2004). 'Seeking Asylum Alone: Treatment of Separated
and Trafficked Children in Need of Refugee Protection'.
International Migration, 42, (1), 141-148.

Bloom, T. (2010). 'Asylum Seekers: Subjects or Objects of
Research?' The American Journal of Bioethics, 10, (2), 59-60.

Bokhari, F. (2008). 'Falling Through the Gaps: Safeguarding
Children Trafficked into the UK', Children & Society, 22, 201-211.

Bowlby, J. (1979) (2005 ed). The Making and Breaking of Affectional
Bonds. Abingdon: Routledge Classics.

British Association of Social Workers. Code of Ethics.

10

Brown, J.D. et al. (2009a). 'Benefits of transcultural fostering', Child & Family Social Work, 15, 276-285, 2010.

Brown, J.D. et al. (2009b). 'Confidence to Foster Across Cultures: Caregiver Perspectives', Journal of Child & Family Studies, 18, 633-642.

Bryman, A. (2008). Social Research Methods, Oxford: Oxford University Press.

Cemlyn, S. & Briskman, L. (2003). 'Asylum, children's rights and social work', Child & Family Social Work, 8, 163-178.

Chase, E. (2009). 'Agency and Silence: Young People Seeking Asylum Alone in the UK',

British Journal of Social Work, Advance Access, September 22, 2009, 1-9, doi:10.1093/bjsw/bcp 103.

Chase, E. et al. (2008). The emotional well-being of young people seeking asylum in the UK, London: British Agencies for Adoption and Fostering.

Children Act 1989

Colton, M. et al. (2006). 'The Recruitment and Retention of Family Foster-Carers: An International and Cross-Cultural Analysis', British Journal of Social Work, 38, 865-884.

Crawford, K. & Walker, J. (2007). Social Work and Human Development. Exeter: Learning Matters Ltd.

Crawley, H. (2009). 'No one gives you a chance to say what you are thinking': finding space for children's agency in the UK asylum system, Area, 42, (2), 162-169, 2010.

Department for Children, Schools and Families. (2010). Working Together to Safeguard Children – A guide to inter-agency working to safeguard and promote the welfare of children.

Department of Health (2003) Guidance on accommodating children in need and their families. Local Authority Circular, (2003) 13.

http://www.dh.gov.uk/dr_consum_dh/groups/dh_digitalassets/@dh/@en/documents/digitalasset/dh_4012756.pdf

[Accessed: 21/08/10]

Department of Health et al. (2000). Framework for the Assessment of Children In Need and their Families.

http://www.dh.gov.uk/prod_consum_dh/groups/dh_digitalassets/@dh/@en/documents/digitalasset/dh_4014430.pdf

[Accessed: 02/07/10]

Denscombe, M. (2007). The Good Research Guide for small scale social research projects.

New York: Open University Press.

Derluyn, I., Broekaert, E. (2008). 'Unaccompanied refugee children and adolescents: the glaring contrast between a legal and a psychological perspective', International Journal of Law and Psychiatry, 31, 318-330.

Fees, B.S. et al. (1998). 'Satisfaction with Foster Parenting: Assessment One Year After Training', Children and Youth Services Review, 20, (4), 347-363.

Fejen, L. (2009). 'The Challenges of Ensuring Protection to Unaccompanied and Separated Children in Composite Flows in Europe', Refugee Survey Quarterly, 27, (4), 63-73.

Fonagy, P. & Target, M. (1997). Attachment and reflective function: Their role in self-organization, Development and Psychopathology, 9, 677-700.

Fostering Network. (2009). The Skills to Foster. London: Fostering Network.

Fox, M. (2002). 'A question of survival: who cares for the carers?' Journal of Social Work Practice, 16, (2), 185-190.

Freedman, J. (2009). 'Protecting Women Asylum Seekers and Refugees: From International Norms to National Protection?' International Migration, 48, (1), 175-198, 2010.

Gilligan, R. (2004). 'Promoting Resilience in Child and Family Social Work: Issues for Social Work Practice, Education and Policy', Social Work Education, 23, (1), 93-104.

Golding, K. & Picken, W. (2004). 'Group work with foster carers caring for children with complex problems', Adoption & Fostering, 28, (1), 25-37.

Guerney, L.F. & Wolfgang, G. (1981). 'Long-Range Evaluation of Effects on Foster Parents of a Foster Parent Skills Training Program, Journal of Clinical Child Psychology, 10, (1), 33-37.

Hampson, R.B. et al. (1983). 'Individual verses Group Training for Foster Carers: Efficiency/Effectiveness Evaluations', Family Relations, 32, (2), 191-201.

Hill-Tout, J., et al. (2003). 'Training foster carers in a preventive approach to children who challenge, Mixed messages from research', Adoption & Fostering, 27, (1), 47-56).

Hodges, M. (2002). 'Three Key Issues for Young Refugees' Mental Health', Transcultural Psychiatry, 39, 196-213.

11

Hopkins, P. & Hill, M. (2010). 'The needs and strengths of unaccompanied asylum-seeking children and young people in Scotland', Child & Family Social Work, 2010, 1-10. doi:10.111/j.1365-2206.2010.00687.x

Home Office – Border & Immigration Agency. (2008). Better Outcomes: The Way Forward – Improving The Care of Unaccompanied Asylum Seeking Children. London: Border & Immigration Agency Communications Directorate.
Home Office – Immigration & Nationality Directorate. (2007).

Planning Better Outcomes and Support for Unaccompanied Asylum Seeking Children (Consultation Paper). London: IND Communications.

Hutchinson, B., et al. (2003). 'Skills protect' – Towards a professional foster care service, Adoption & Fostering, 27, (3), 8-13.

Jackson, L.J. et al. (2009). 'Exploring spirituality among youth in foster care: findings from the Casey field Office Mental Health Study', Child & Family Social Work, 15, 107-117, 2010.

Johnson, S.B., Blum, R.W., and Giedd, J.N. 'Adolescent Maturity and the Brain: The Promise and Pitfalls in Adolescent Health Policy', Journal of Adolescent Health, 2009, 45) 216-221.

Kholi R.K.S. (2008). 'Unaccompanied asylum-seeking and refugee children and their transition into care', in Direct Work – Social work with children and young people in care, (eds.) B. Luckock & M. Lefevre. UK: British Agencies for Adoption and Fostering.

Kholi, R.K.S. et al. (2007). Working with Unaccompanied Asylum Seeking Children. Hampshire: Palgrave MacMillan.

Kholi, R.K.S. (2005). 'The Sound of Silence: Listening to What Unaccompanied Asylum Seeking Children Say and Do Not Say', British Journal of Social Work, 36, 707-721.

Kholi, R.K.S, & Mather, R. (2003). 'Promoting psychological well-being in unaccompanied asylum seeking young people in the United Kingdom', Child & Family Social Work, 8, 201-212.

Kidane, S. & Amarena, P. (2004) Fostering Unaccompanied Asylum Seeking and Refugee Children – A Training Course for Foster Carers. London: British Agencies for Adoption and Fostering.

Kidane, S. (2001). Food, Shelter and Half a Chance, Assessing the needs of unaccompanied asylum seeking and refugee children. London: British Agencies for Adoption and Fostering.

Lay, M. & Papadopoulous, I. (2009). 'Sexual maltreatment of unaccompanied asylum-seeking minors from the Horn of Africa: A mixed method study focusing on vulnerability and prevention', Child Abuse & Neglect, 33, 728-738.

Luster, T. et al. (2009). 'The Experiences of Sudanese Unaccompanied Minors in Foster Care', Journal of Family Psychology, 23, (3), 386-395.

Macdonald, G. & Turner, W. (2005). 'An Experiment in Helping Foster-Carers Manage Challenging Behaviour', British Journal of Social Work, 35, 1265-1282.

Maegusuku-Hewett, T. et al. (2007). 'Refugee Children in Wales: Coping and Adaptation in the Face of Adversity', Children & Society, 21, 309-321.

Martin, F. & Curran. J. (2007). 'Separated Children: A comparison of the Treatment of Separated Child Refugees Entering Australia and Canada', International Journal of Refugee Law, 19, 3), 440-470.

Minnis, H. et al. (2001). 'Mental health and foster carer training', Archives of Disease in Childhood, 84, 302-306.

Mitchell, F. (2003). 'The social services response to unaccompanied children in England', Child & Family Social Work, 8, 179-189.

National Evaluation of the Children's Fund

http://publications.education.gov.uk/eOrderingDownload/RB780.pdf

Ni Raghallaigh, M. & Gilligan, R. (2009). 'Active survival in the lives of unaccompanied minors: coping strategies, resilience, and the relevance of religion', Child & Family Social Work, 15, 226-237, 2010.

Okitkpi, T. & Aymer, C. (2003). 'Social work with African refugee children and their families', Child and Family Social Work, 8, 213-222.

Puddy, R.W. & Jackson, Y. (2003). 'The Development of Parenting Skills in Foster Parent Training', Children and Youth Services Review, 25, (12), 987-1013.

Robinson, L. (2007). Cross-cultural child development for social workers, Hampshire: Palgrave Macmillan.

Schofield, G. (2010) Expert paper on Support and training for foster carers.

http://www.nice.org.uk/nicemedia/live/11879/47434/47434.pdf

Sunderland, M. The Science of Parenting. 2006. London: Dorling Kindersley Ltd.

Thomas, S. et al. (2003). 'I was running away from death'- the pre-flight experiences of unaccompanied asylum seeking children in the UK, Child: Care, Health & Development, 30, (2), 113-122.

Thomas, S. & Byford, S. (2003). 'Research with unaccompanied children seeking asylum', British Medical Journal, 327, 1400-1402.

Titterington, L. (1990). 'Foster Care Training: A Comprehensive Approach'. Child Welfare, 69, 157-165.

The Fostering Services Regulations 2002. Norwich: The Stationery Office Limited.

Wade, J. et al. (2009-2011). Fostering unaccompanied asylum-seeking and refugee children.

www.rip.org.uk

Research in Practice [Accessed: 24/08/10]

Warman, A., et al. (2006). 'Learning from each other: Process and outcomes in the Fostering Changes programme', Adoption & Fostering, 30, (3), 17-28.

Warwick, I., et al. (2006). 'My Life in Huddersfield: Supporting Young Asylum Seekers and Refugees to Record Their Experiences Living in Huddersfield', Social Work Education, 25, (2), 129-137.

Zion, D., et al. (2010). 'Returning to History: The Ethics of Researching Asylum Seeker Health in Australia', The American Journal of Bioethics, 10, (2), 48-56, 2010.

Printed in Great Britain
by Amazon

28294234R00066